Cute Little Fish
Publishing

This is a multi-activity book: copy the picture, trace it, color it and draw your own composition. At the end of the book you will find extra grid by grid and freehand pages to practice. All together will give your child many hours of creative fun.

Each image is divided into small parts within the grid. By learning to redraw small sections, your child can quickly learn the entire drawing. When the drawing is finished - you can color it beautifully!

Drawings vary in level of details and difficulty. It's a great book for beginners of all ages not just kids.

This children's drawing book gives you 35 designs to learn, draw and practice. Let's draw cute, sweet and silly monsters.
Draw and have fun !

☆☆☆☆☆

We hope you enjoy this book!
We'd deeply appreciate if you could support us in our small independent publishing business by leaving a review on Amazon

☆☆☆☆☆

Cute Little Fish
Publishing

Before you start

All you need is a pencil and an eraser. And a set of crayons to color with. Make sure your pencil and crayons are prepared and sharpened properly. When drawing a picture using the grid-by-grid method, focus on the element you are currently drawing. Choose the top left grid where the picture starts and then move step by step (grid by grid) to the last element - the bottom right grid.

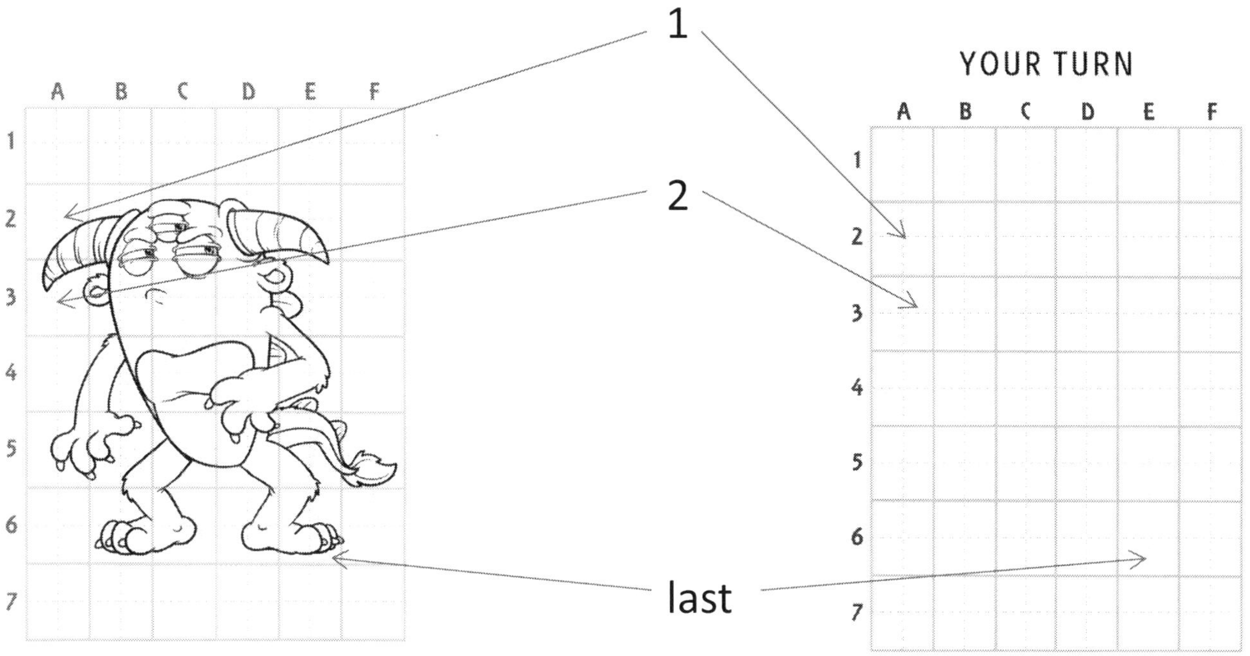

Hints and tips

1. Always start with a pencil and use light strokes
2. You can always erase unwanted lines or, if you are satisfied with the effect, bold them
3. Take your time. Focus on the part you are currently drawing
4. First sketch the outline and then color it in. Bold the lines and add your details
5. Practice on the other pages - trace the picture and make a freehand masterpiece. Color them too
6. At the end of the book you will find extra grid by grid and freehand pages to practice

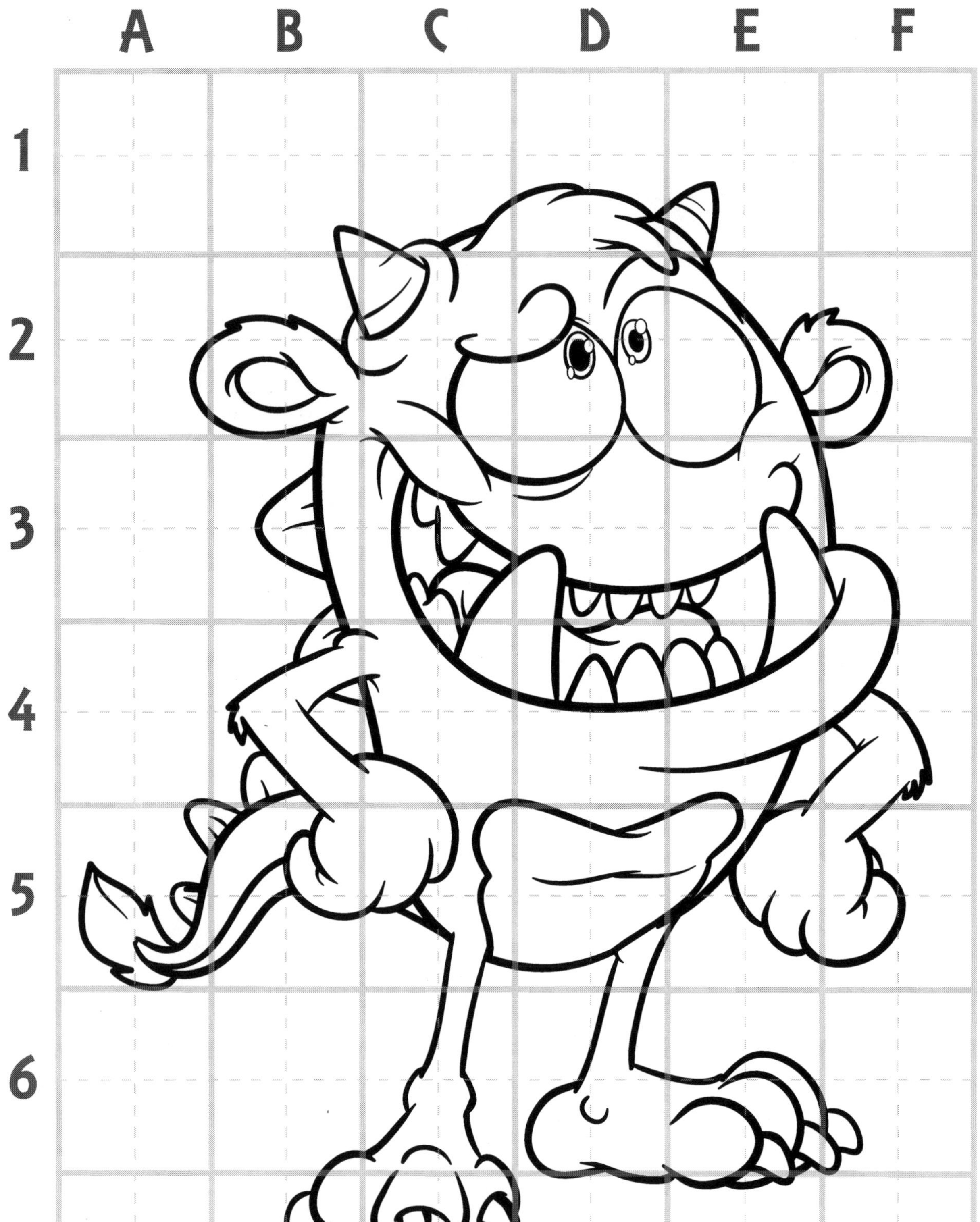
A B C D E F
1
2
3
4
5
6
7

YOUR TURN

	A	B	C	D	E	F
1						
2						
3						
4						
5						
6						
7						

TRACE IT

FREEHAND PRACTICE

A B C D E F
1
2
3
4
5
6
7

YOUR TURN

	A	B	C	D	E	F
1						
2						
3						
4						
5						
6						
7						

TRACE IT

FREEHAND PRACTICE

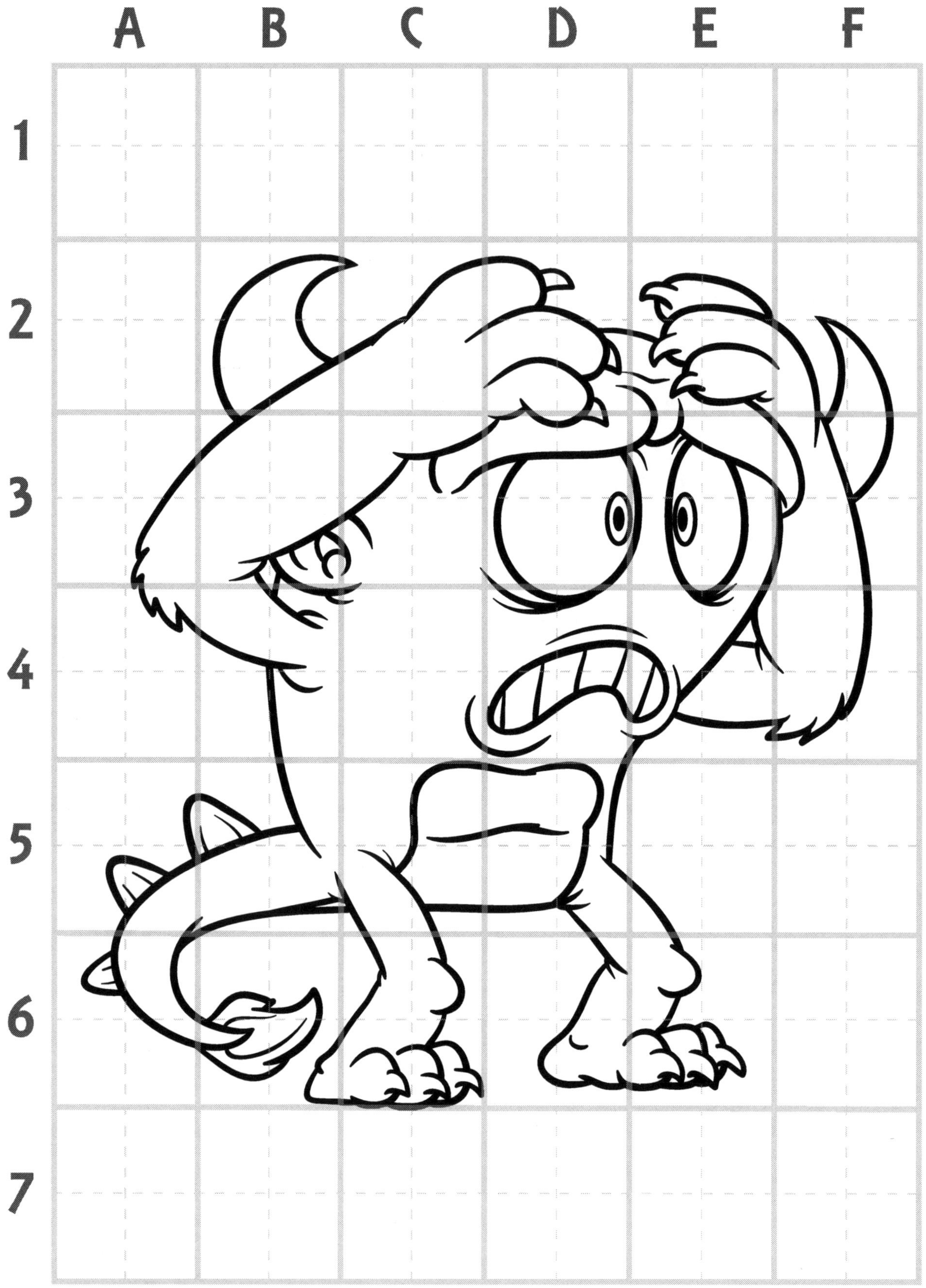
A B C D E F
1
2
3
4
5
6
7

YOUR TURN

	A	B	C	D	E	F
1						
2						
3						
4						
5						
6						
7						

TRACE IT

FREEHAND PRACTICE

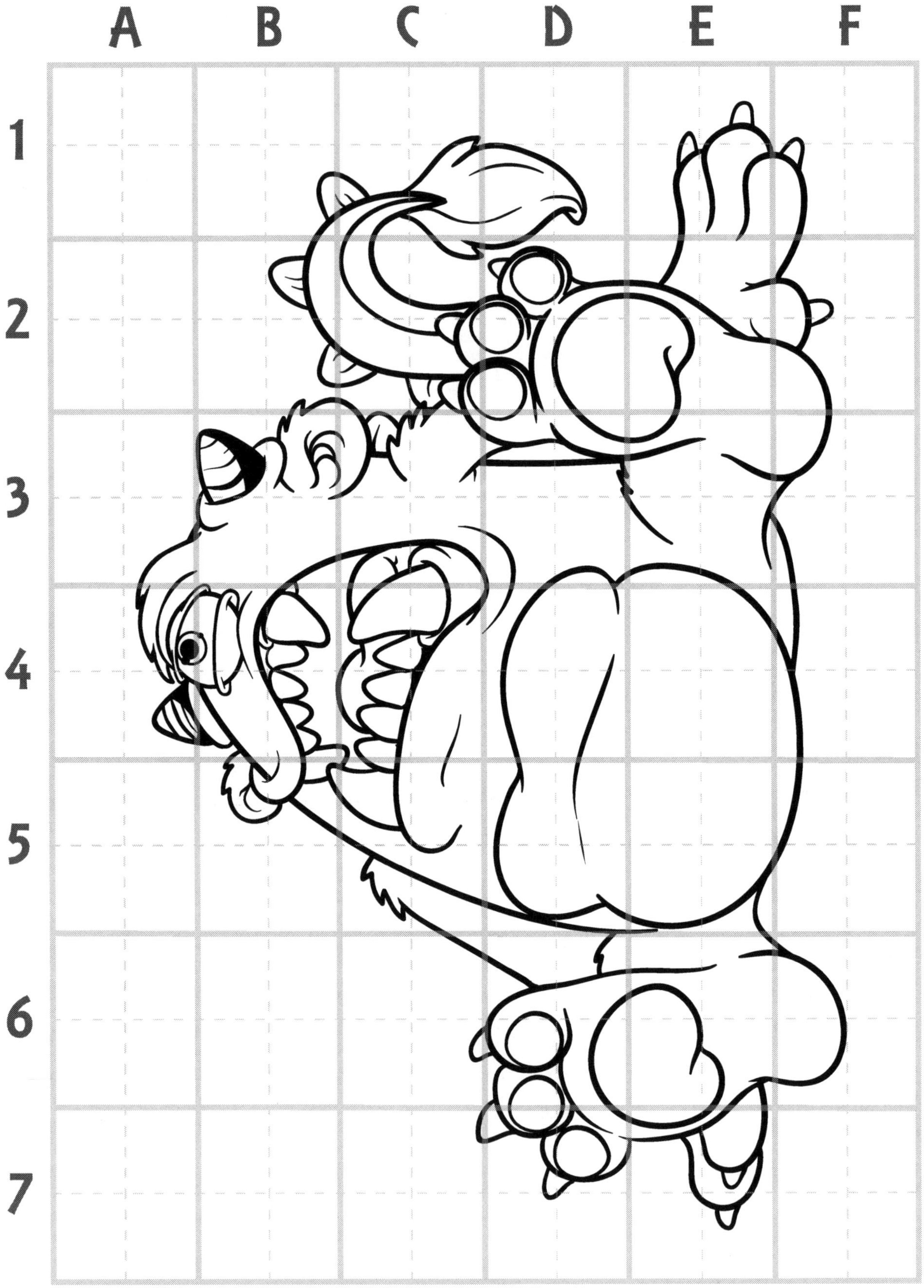
A
B
C
D
E
F
1
2
3
4
5
6
7

YOUR TURN

	A	B	C	D	E	F
1						
2						
3						
4						
5						
6						
7						

TRACE IT

FREEHAND PRACTICE

A B C D E F
1 2 3 4 5 6 7

YOUR TURN

	A	B	C	D	E	F
1						
2						
3						
4						
5						
6						
7						

TRACE IT

FREEHAND PRACTICE

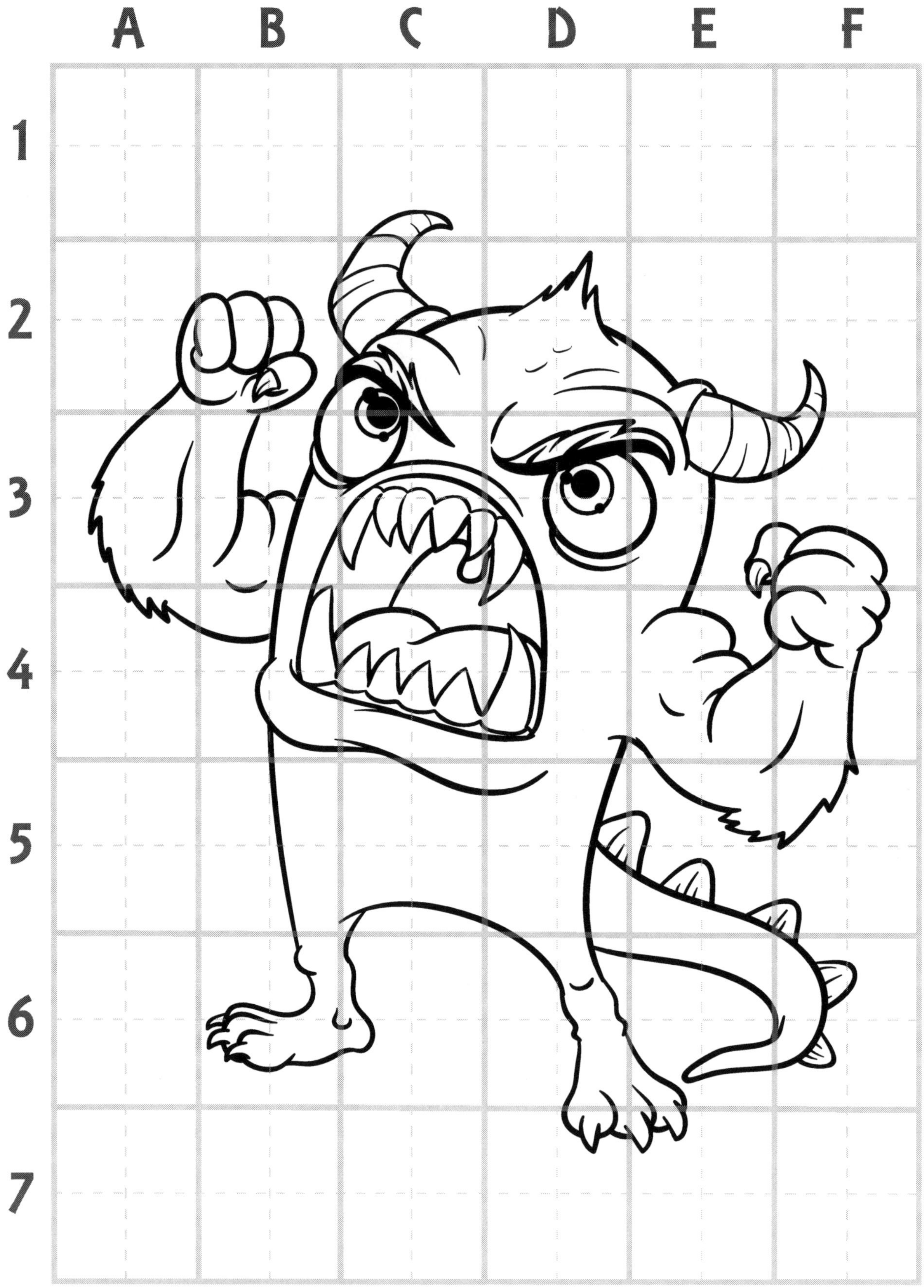
A B C D E F
1
2
3
4
5
6
7

YOUR TURN

	A	B	C	D	E	F
1						
2						
3						
4						
5						
6						
7						

TRACE IT

FREEHAND PRACTICE

A
B
C
D
E
F
1
2
3
4
5
6
7

YOUR TURN

	A	B	C	D	E	F
1						
2						
3						
4						
5						
6						
7						

TRACE IT

FREEHAND PRACTICE

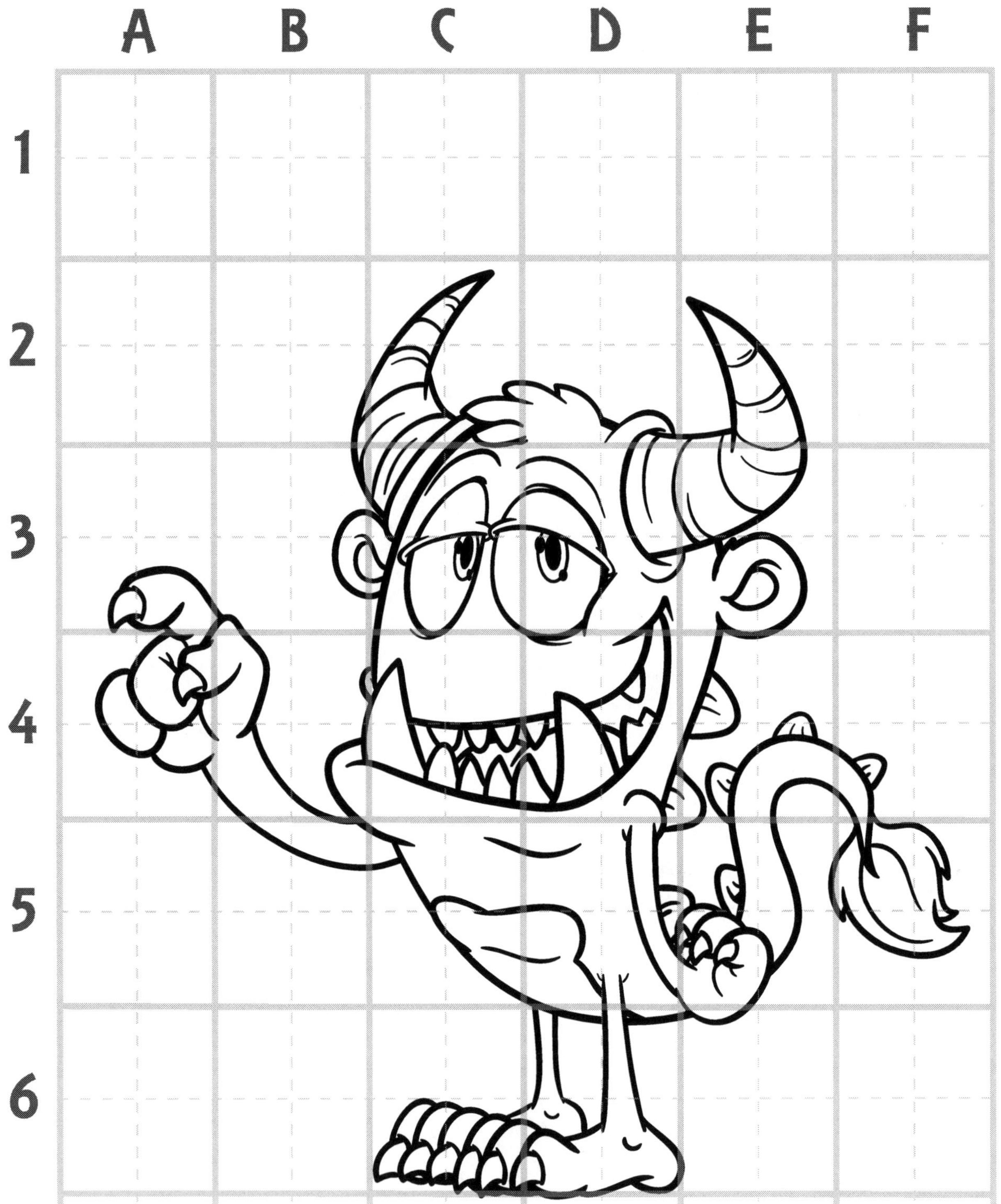
A B C D E F
1
2
3
4
5
6
7

YOUR TURN

	A	B	C	D	E	F
1						
2						
3						
4						
5						
6						
7						

TRACE IT

FREEHAND PRACTICE

A B C D E F
1
2
3
4
5
6
7

YOUR TURN

	A	B	C	D	E	F
1						
2						
3						
4						
5						
6						
7						

TRACE IT

FREEHAND PRACTICE

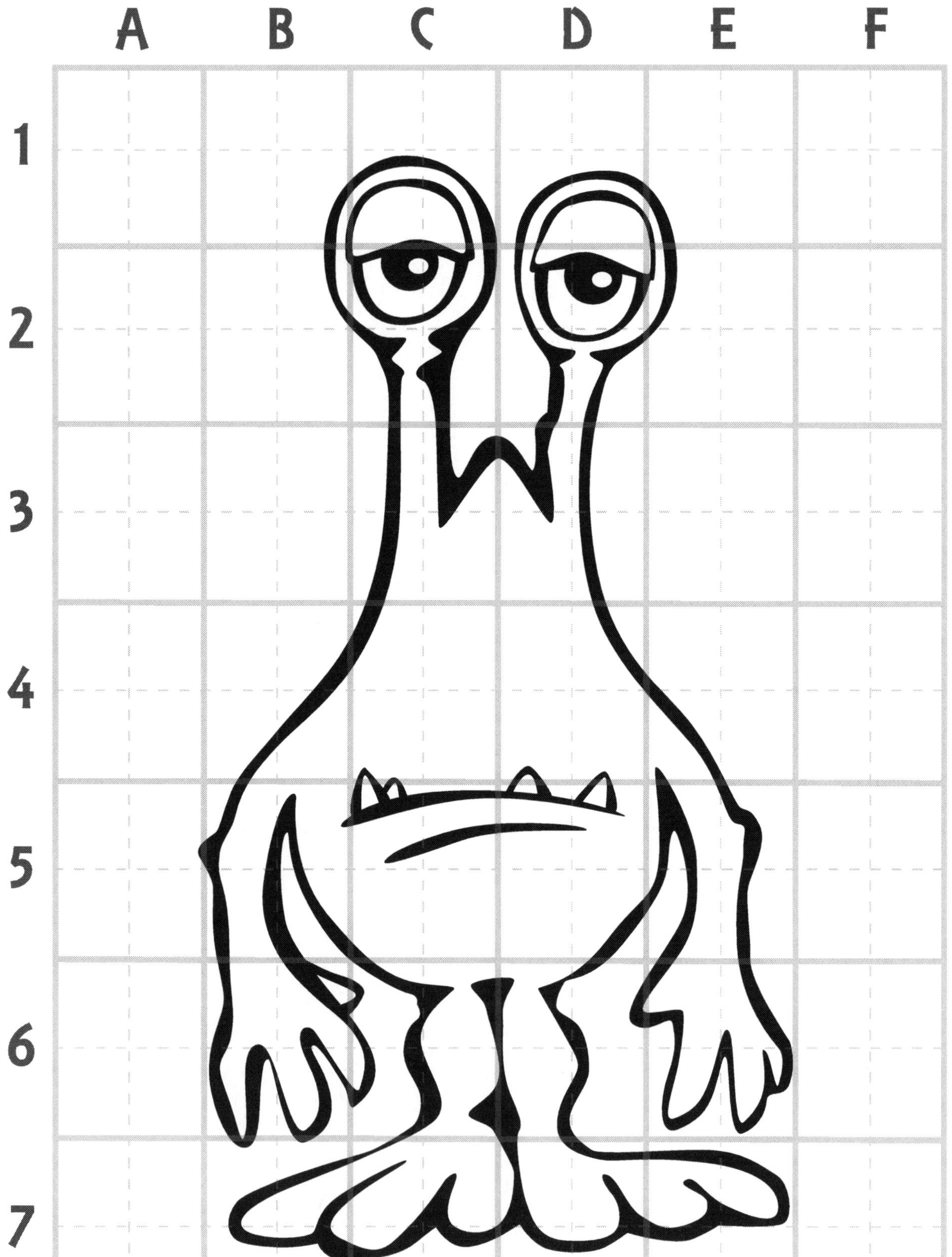
A B C D E F
1
2
3
4
5
6
7

YOUR TURN

	A	B	C	D	E	F
1						
2						
3						
4						
5						
6						
7						

TRACE IT

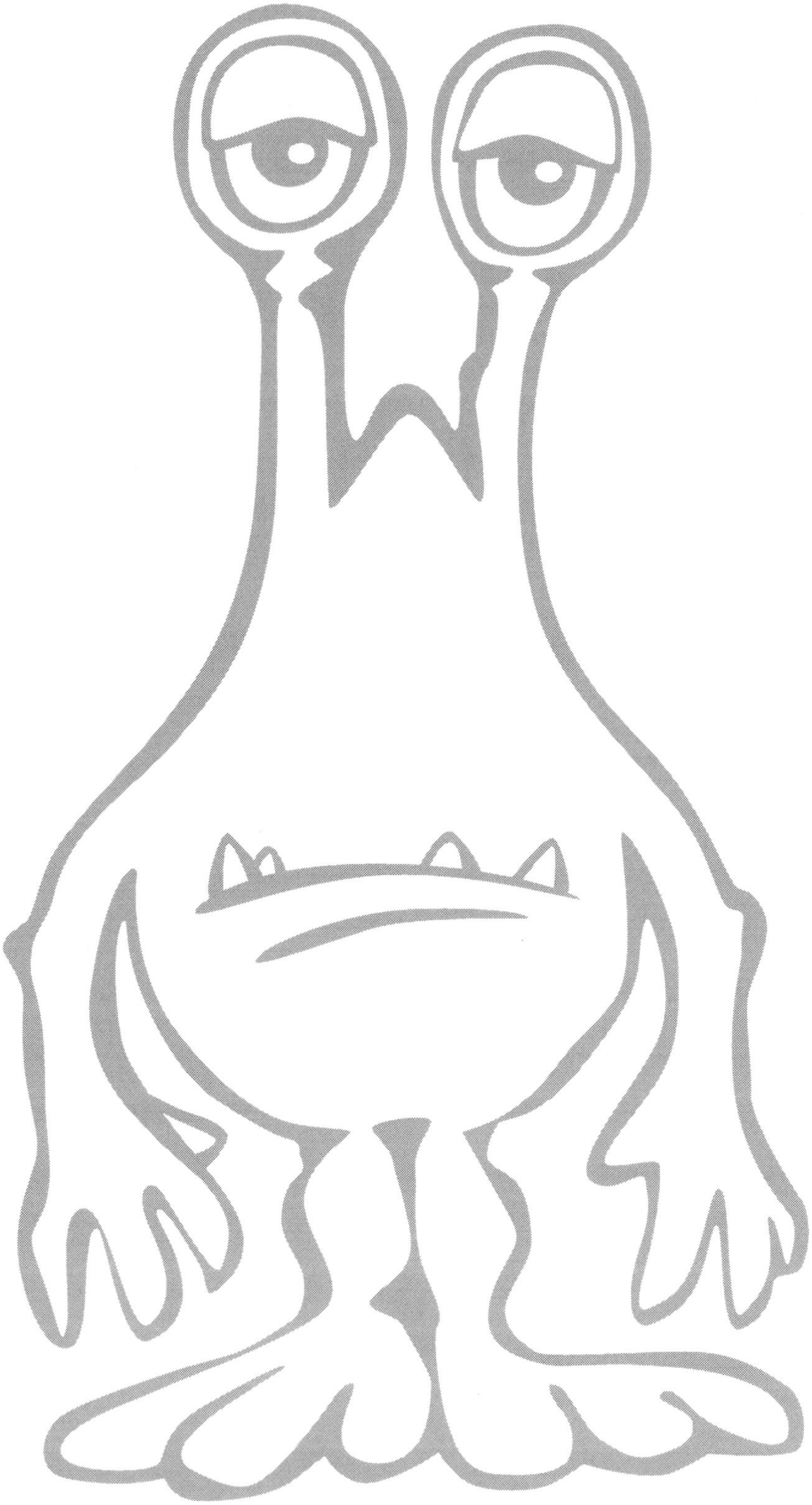

FREEHAND PRACTICE

A
B
C
D
E
F
1
2
3
4
5
6
7

YOUR TURN

	A	B	C	D	E	F
1						
2						
3						
4						
5						
6						
7						

TRACE IT

FREEHAND PRACTICE

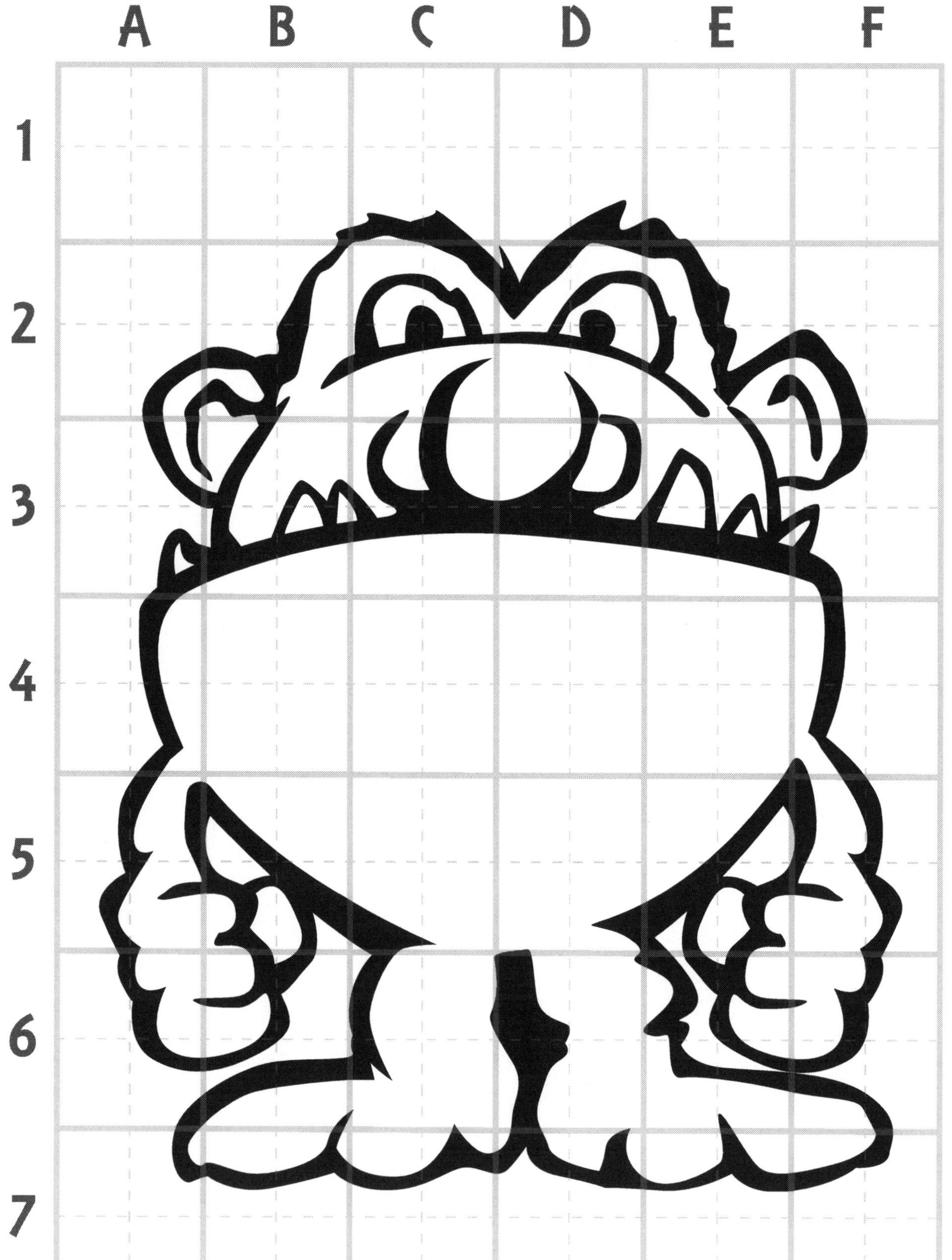
A B C D E F
1
2
3
4
5
6
7

YOUR TURN

	A	B	C	D	E	F
1						
2						
3						
4						
5						
6						
7						

TRACE IT

FREEHAND PRACTICE

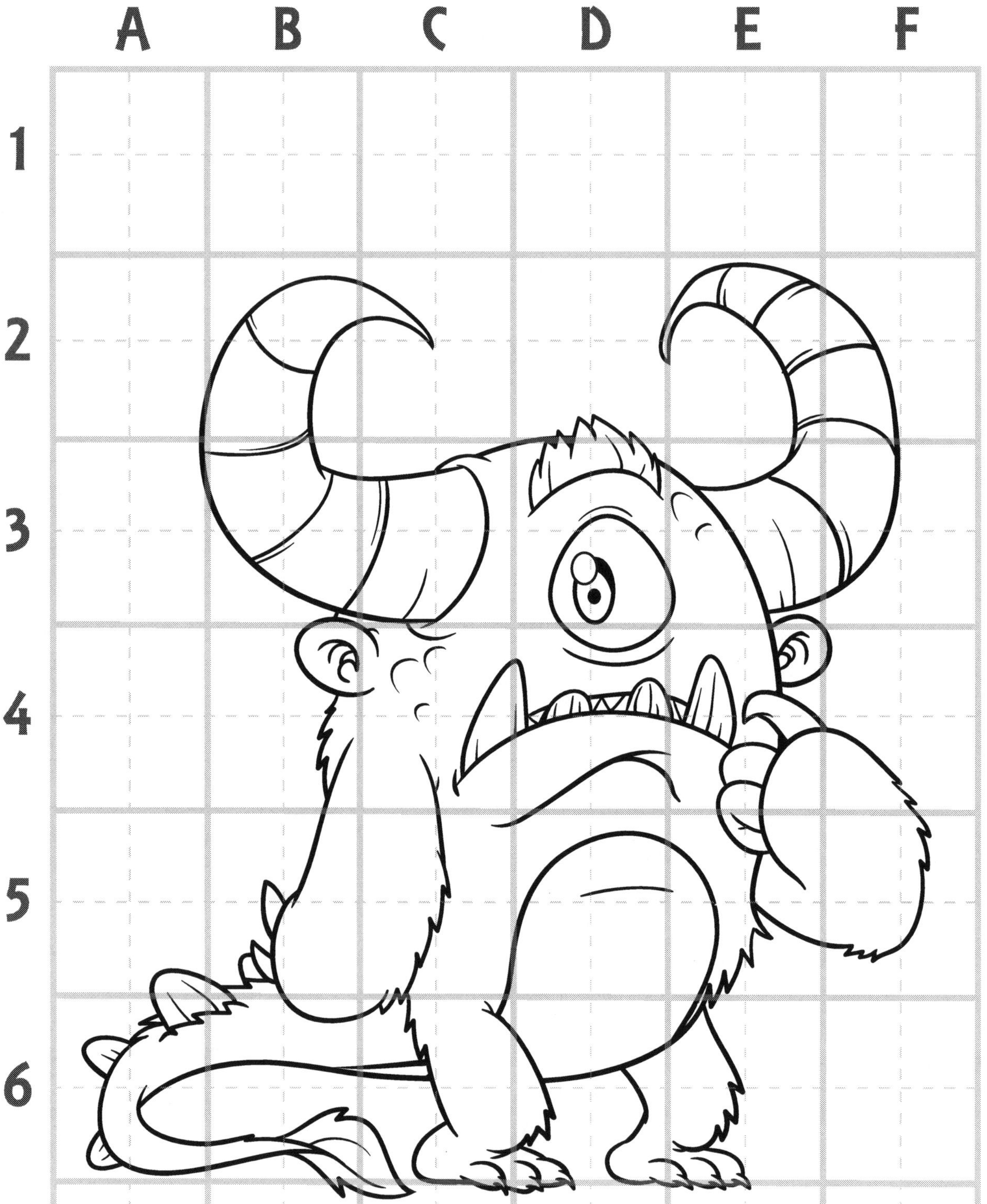
A
B
C
D
E
F
1
2
3
4
5
6
7

YOUR TURN

	A	B	C	D	E	F
1						
2						
3						
4						
5						
6						
7						

TRACE IT

FREEHAND PRACTICE

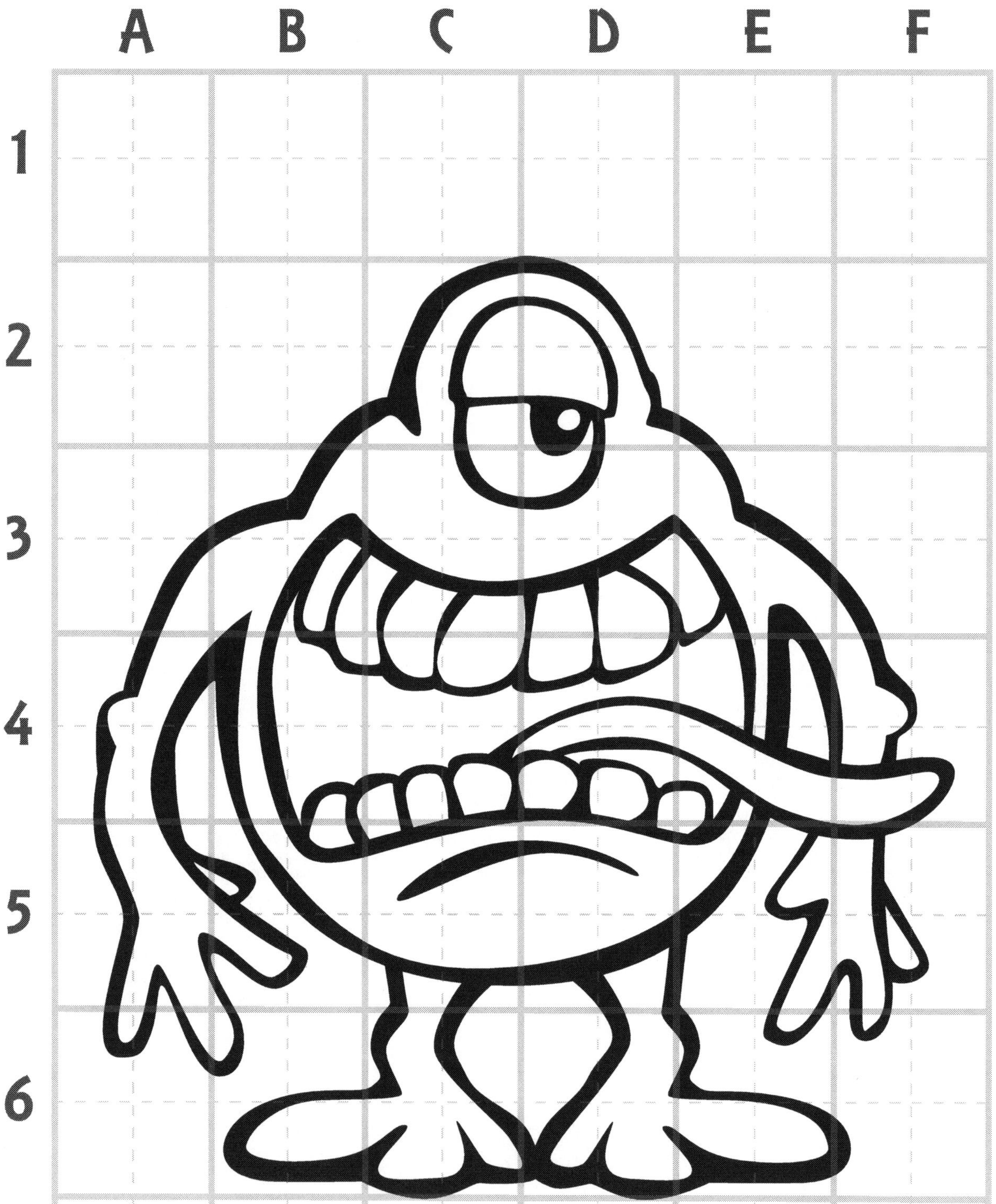
A B C D E F
1
2
3
4
5
6
7

YOUR TURN

	A	B	C	D	E	F
1						
2						
3						
4						
5						
6						
7						

TRACE IT

FREEHAND PRACTICE

A
B
C
D
E
F
1
2
3
4
5
6
7

YOUR TURN

	A	B	C	D	E	F
1						
2						
3						
4						
5						
6						
7						

TRACE IT

FREEHAND PRACTICE

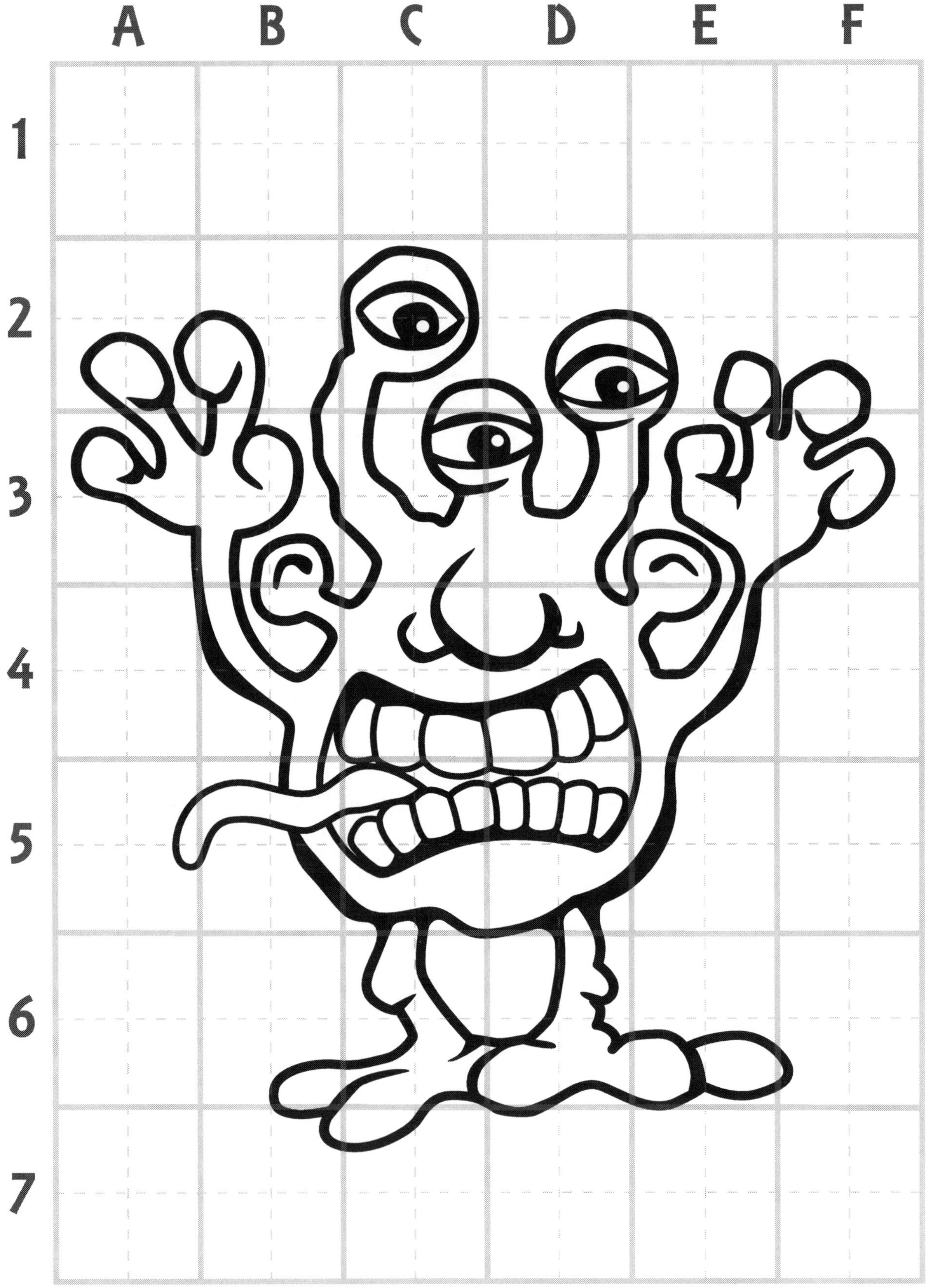
A
B
C
D
E
F
1
2
3
4
5
6
7

YOUR TURN

	A	B	C	D	E	F
1						
2						
3						
4						
5						
6						
7						

TRACE IT

FREEHAND PRACTICE

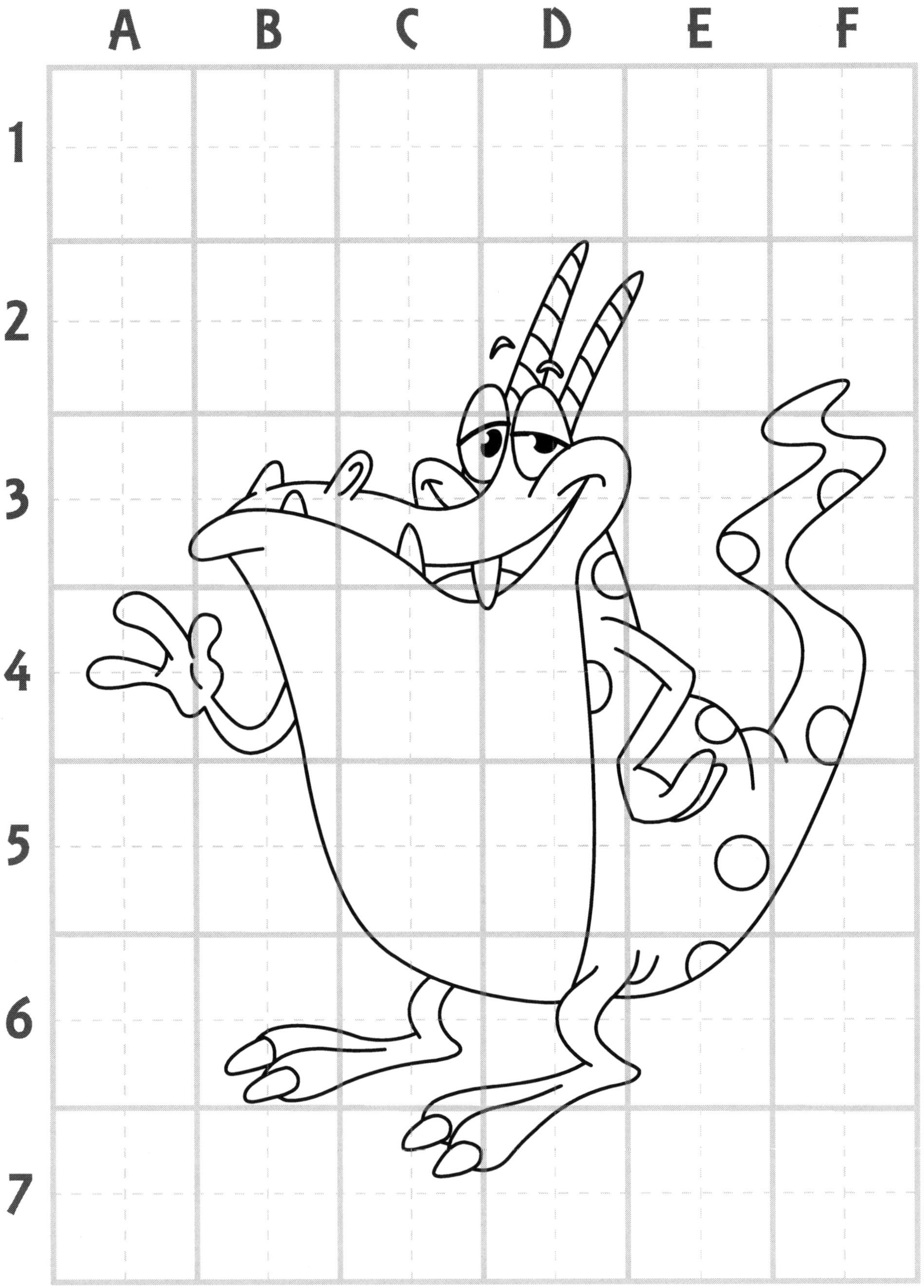
A B C D E F
1
2
3
4
5
6
7

YOUR TURN

	A	B	C	D	E	F
1						
2						
3						
4						
5						
6						
7						

TRACE IT

FREEHAND PRACTICE

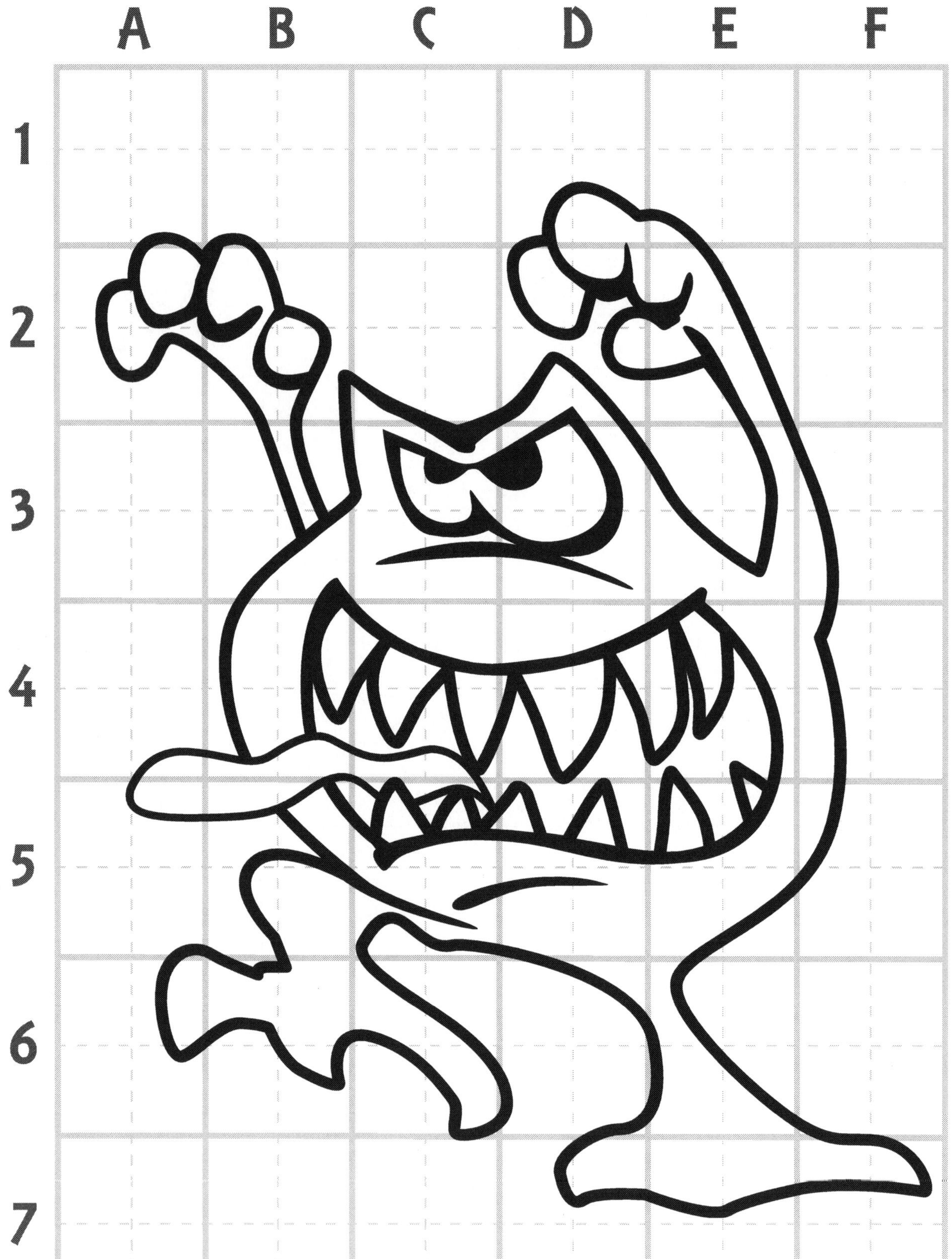
A B C D E F
1
2
3
4
5
6
7

YOUR TURN

	A	B	C	D	E	F
1						
2						
3						
4						
5						
6						
7						

TRACE IT

FREEHAND PRACTICE

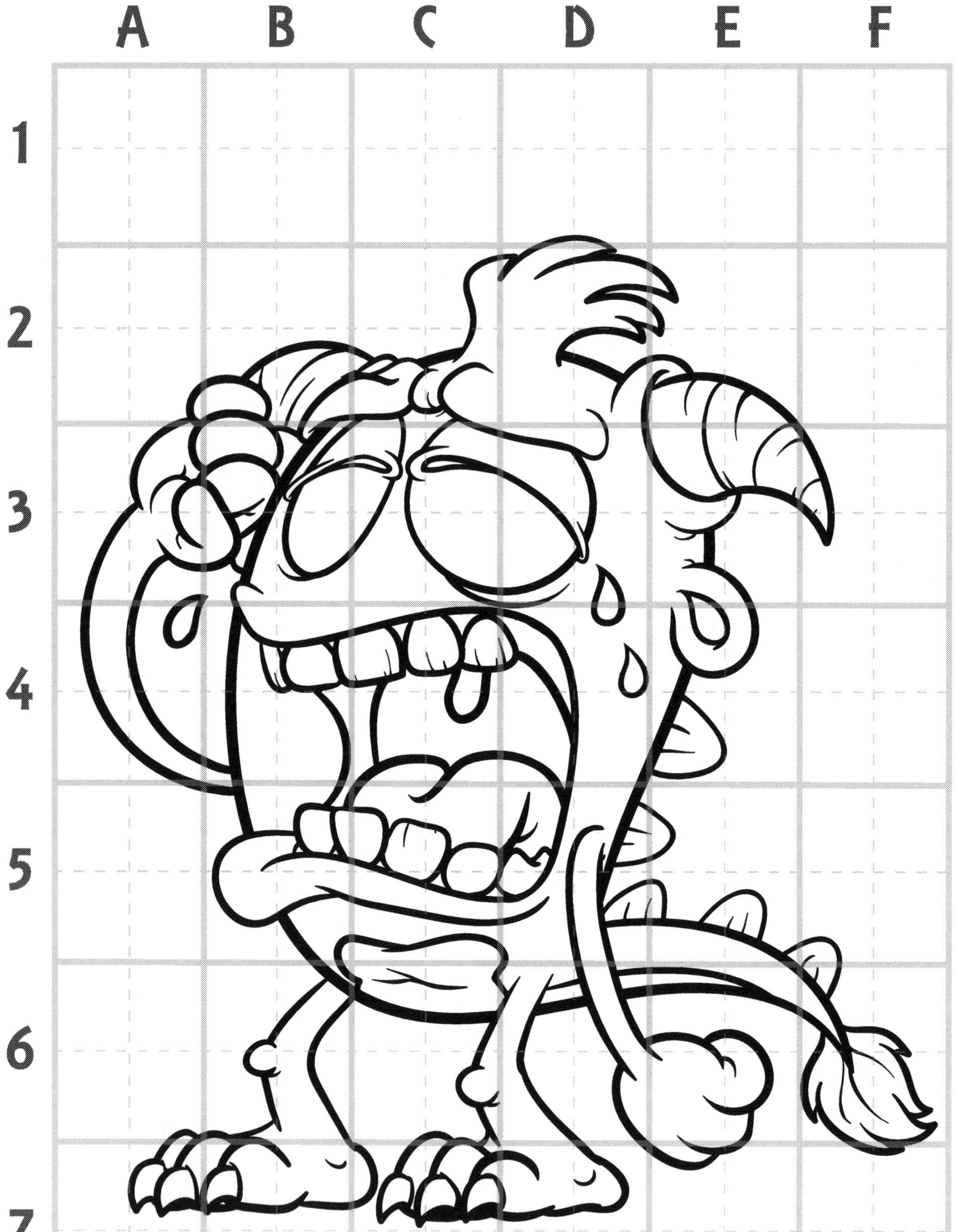
A B C D E F
1 2 3 4 5 6 7

YOUR TURN

	A	B	C	D	E	F
1						
2						
3						
4						
5						
6						
7						

TRACE IT

FREEHAND PRACTICE

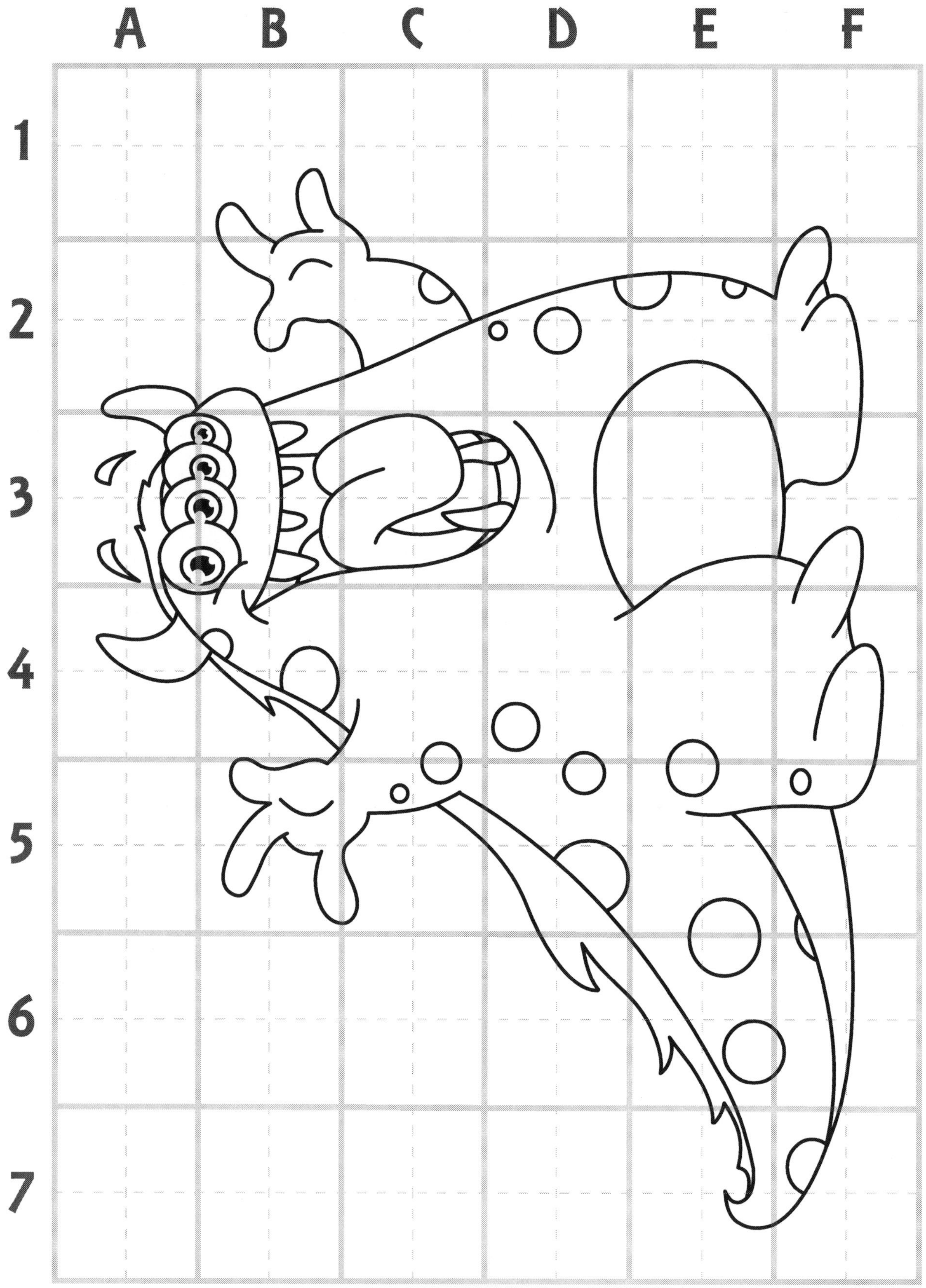
A
B
C
D
E
F
1
2
3
4
5
6
7

YOUR TURN

	A	B	C	D	E	F
1						
2						
3						
4						
5						
6						
7						

TRACE IT

FREEHAND PRACTICE

A B C D E F
1 2 3 4 5 6 7

YOUR TURN

	A	B	C	D	E	F
1						
2						
3						
4						
5						
6						
7						

TRACE IT

FREEHAND PRACTICE

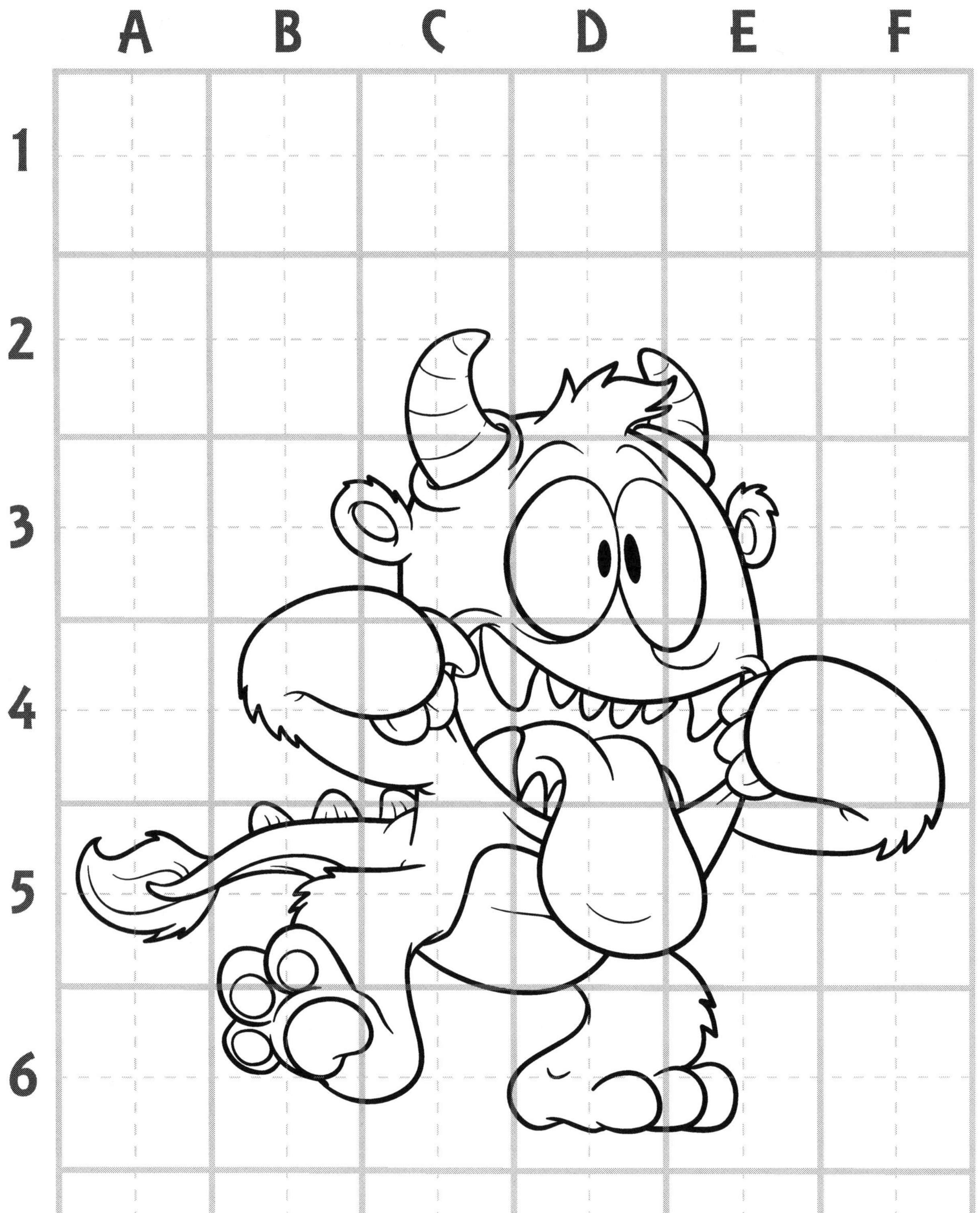
A B C D E F
1 2 3 4 5 6 7

YOUR TURN

	A	B	C	D	E	F
1						
2						
3						
4						
5						
6						
7						

TRACE IT

FREEHAND PRACTICE

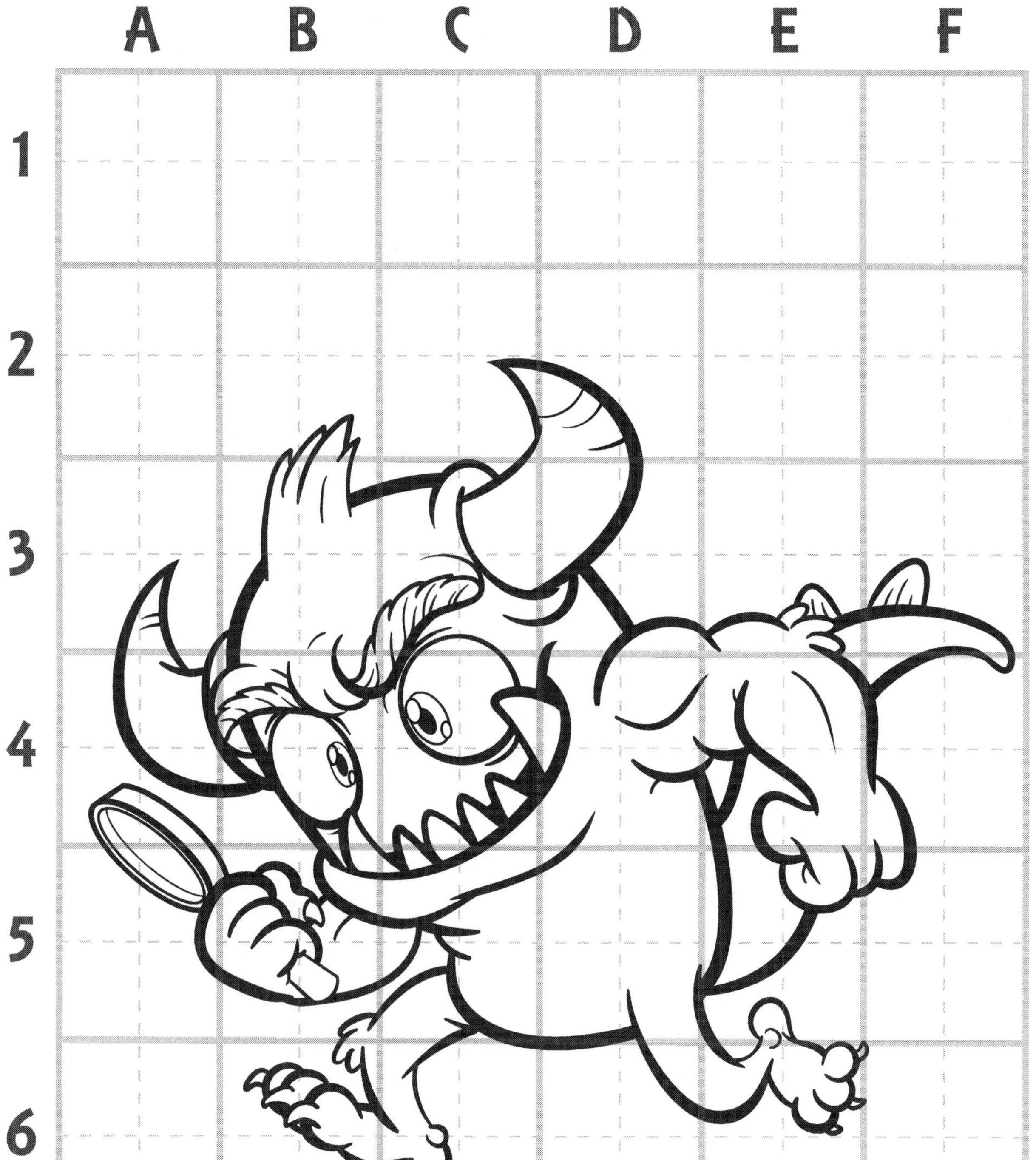
A
B
C
D
E
F
1
2
3
4
5
6
7

YOUR TURN

	A	B	C	D	E	F
1						
2						
3						
4						
5						
6						
7						

TRACE IT

FREEHAND PRACTICE

A B C D E F
1
2
3
4
5
6
7

YOUR TURN

	A	B	C	D	E	F
1						
2						
3						
4						
5						
6						
7						

TRACE IT

FREEHAND PRACTICE

A B C D E F
1 2 3 4 5 6 7

YOUR TURN

	A	B	C	D	E	F
1						
2						
3						
4						
5						
6						
7						

TRACE IT

FREEHAND PRACTICE

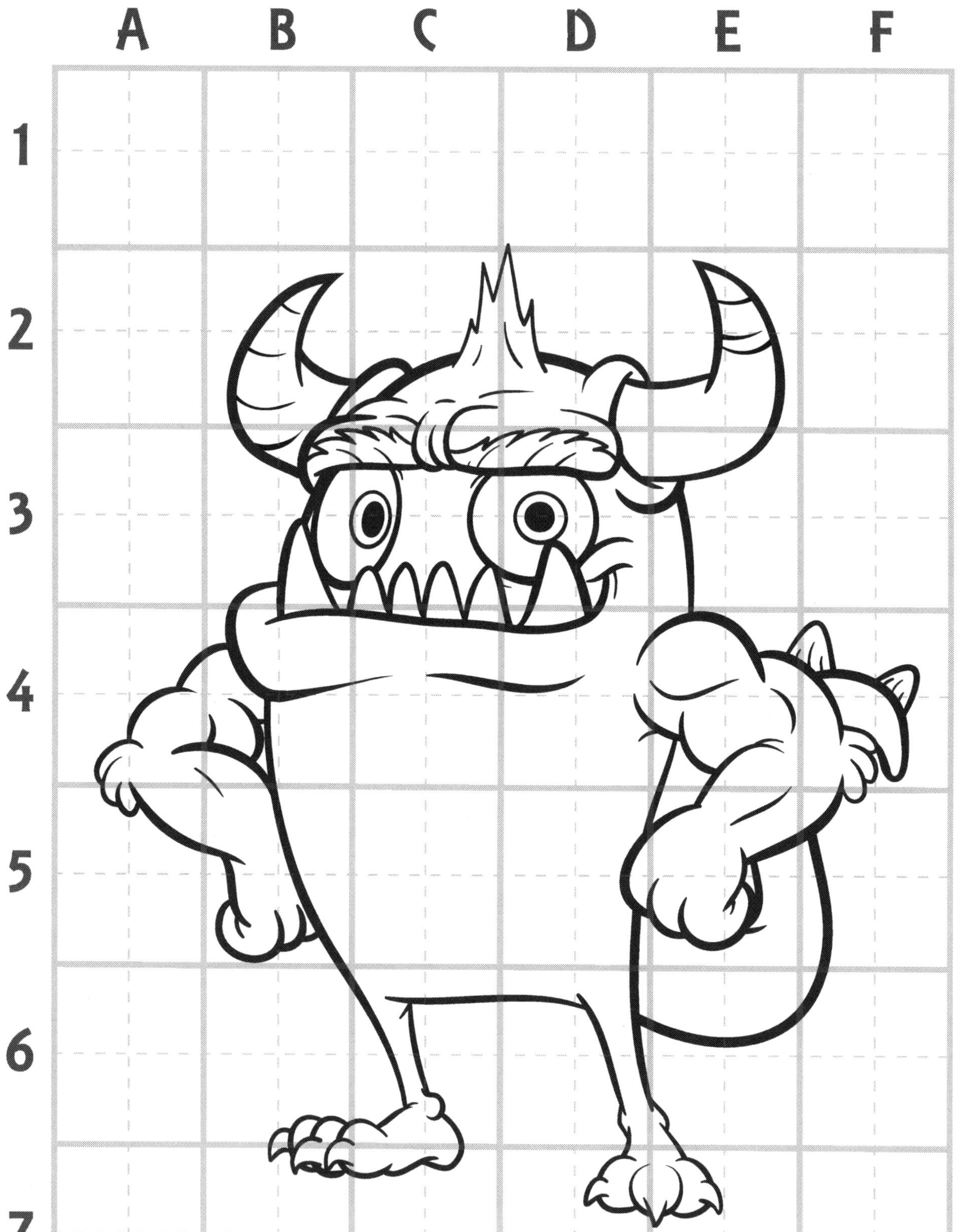
A
B
C
D
E
F
1
2
3
4
5
6
7

YOUR TURN

	A	B	C	D	E	F
1						
2						
3						
4						
5						
6						
7						

TRACE IT

FREEHAND PRACTICE

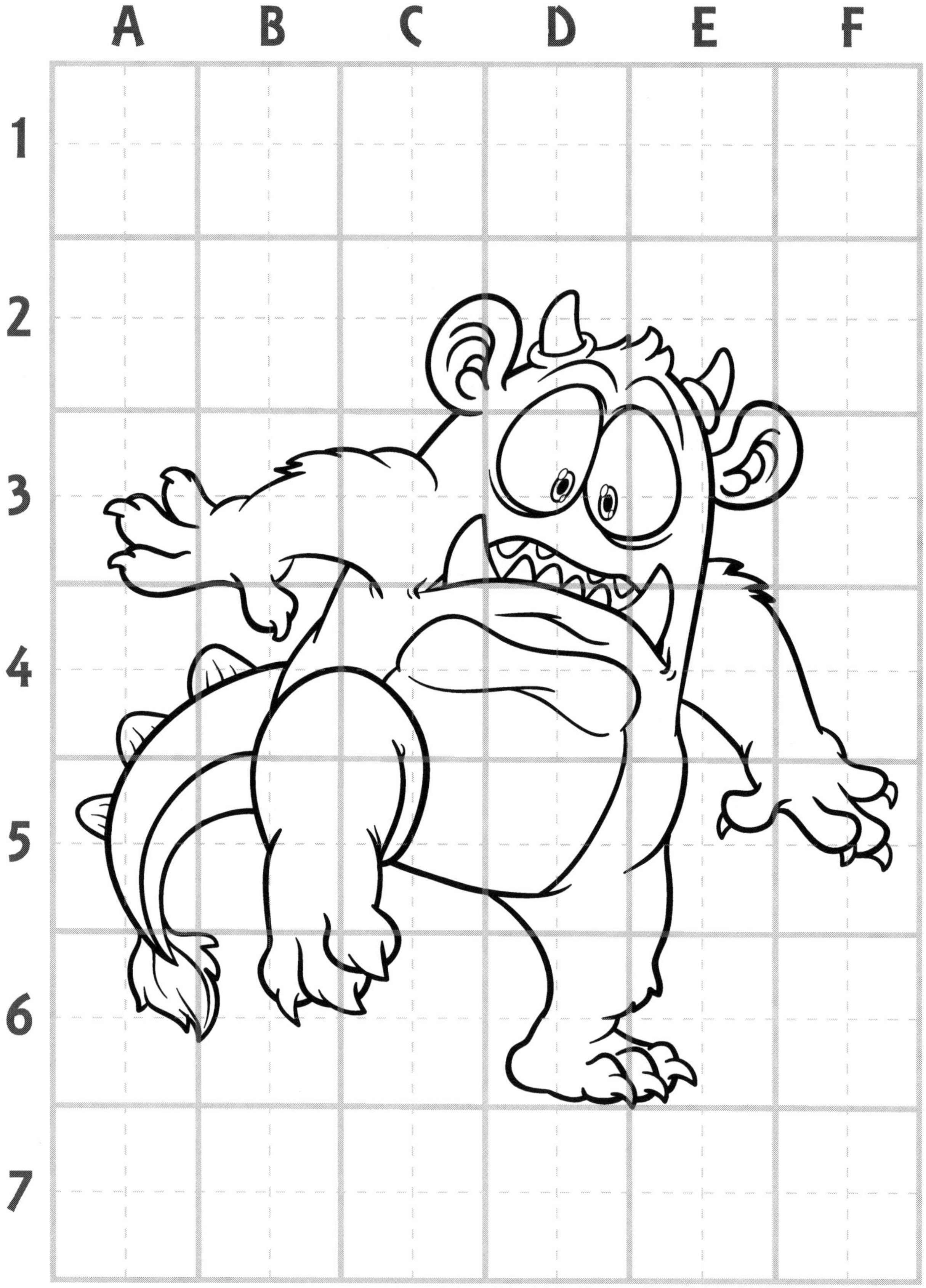
A B C D E F
1
2
3
4
5
6
7

YOUR TURN

	A	B	C	D	E	F
1						
2						
3						
4						
5						
6						
7						

TRACE IT

FREEHAND PRACTICE

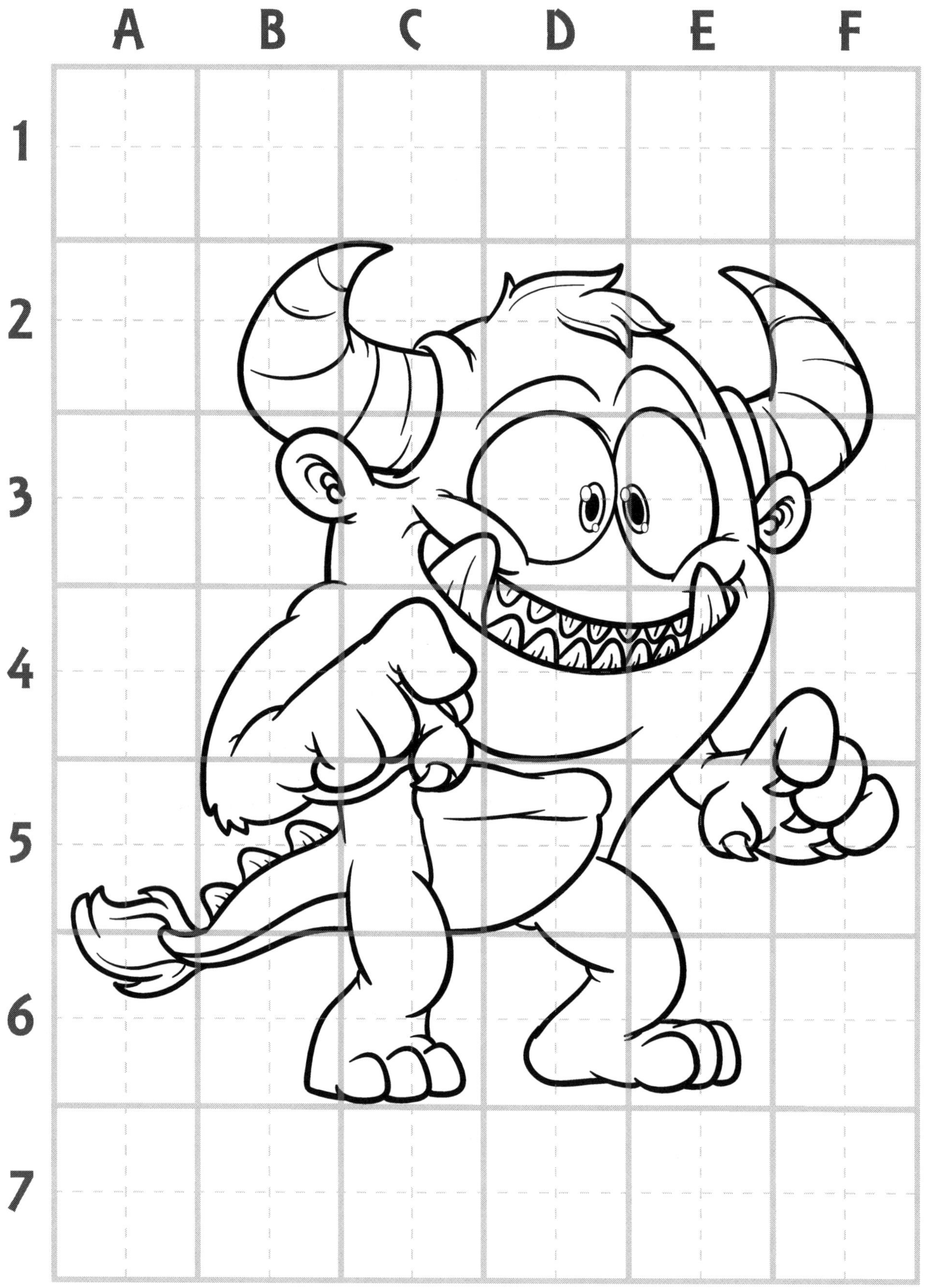
A
B
C
D
E
F
1
2
3
4
5
6
7

YOUR TURN

	A	B	C	D	E	F
1						
2						
3						
4						
5						
6						
7						

TRACE IT

FREEHAND PRACTICE

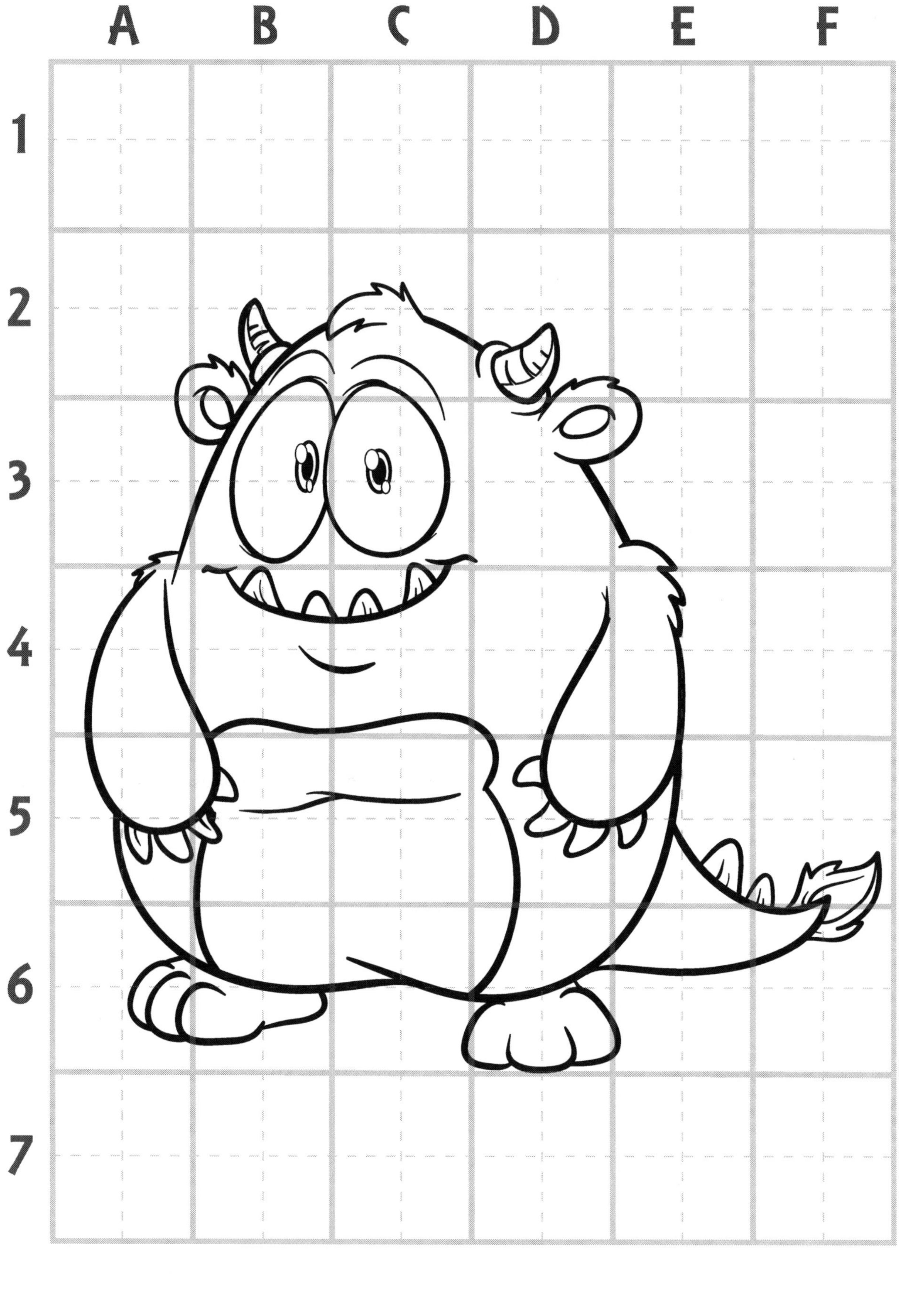
A B C D E F
1
2
3
4
5
6
7

YOUR TURN

	A	B	C	D	E	F
1						
2						
3						
4						
5						
6						
7						

TRACE IT

FREEHAND PRACTICE

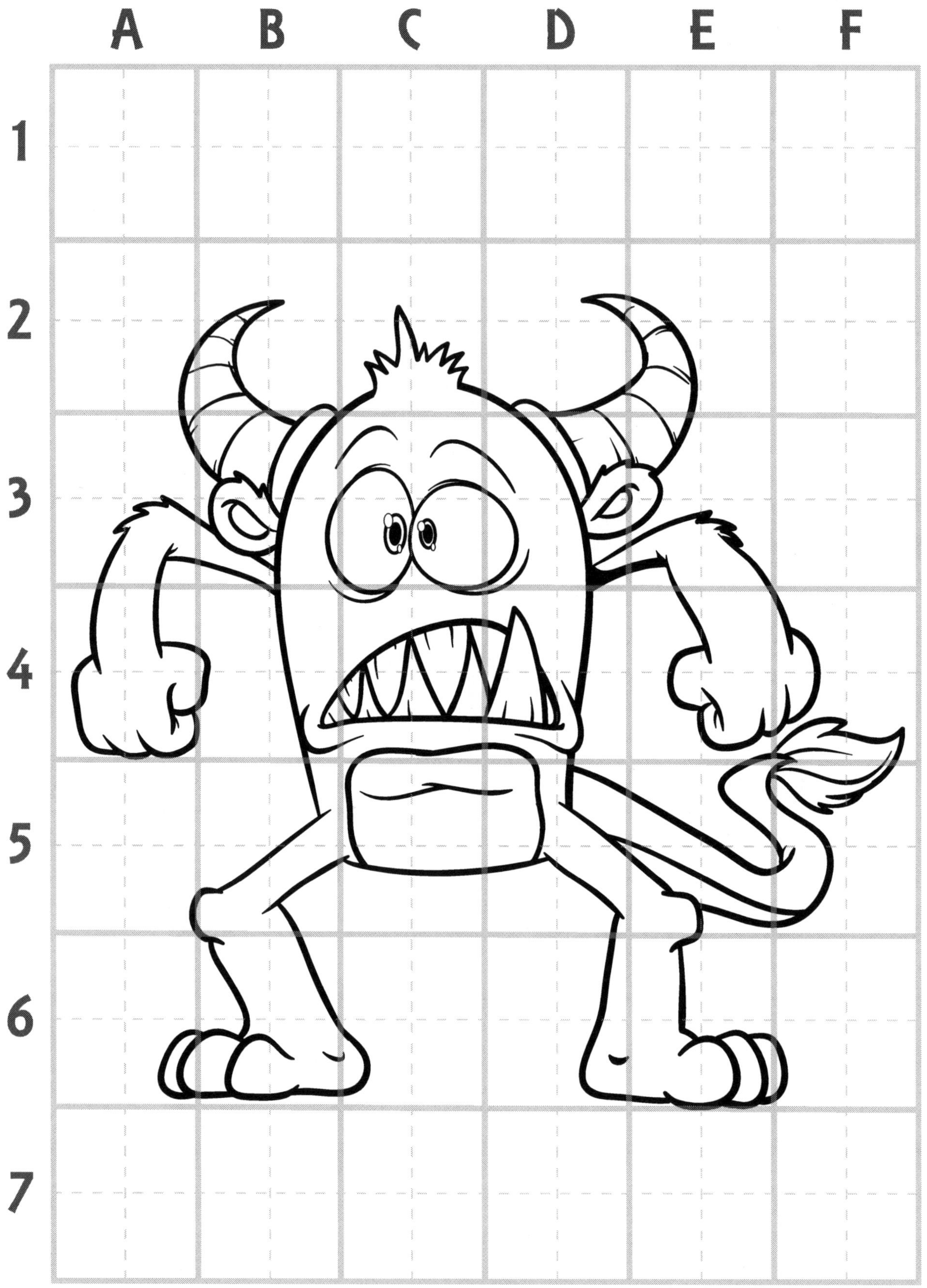
A B C D E F
1 2 3 4 5 6 7

YOUR TURN

	A	B	C	D	E	F
1						
2						
3						
4						
5						
6						
7						

TRACE IT

FREEHAND PRACTICE

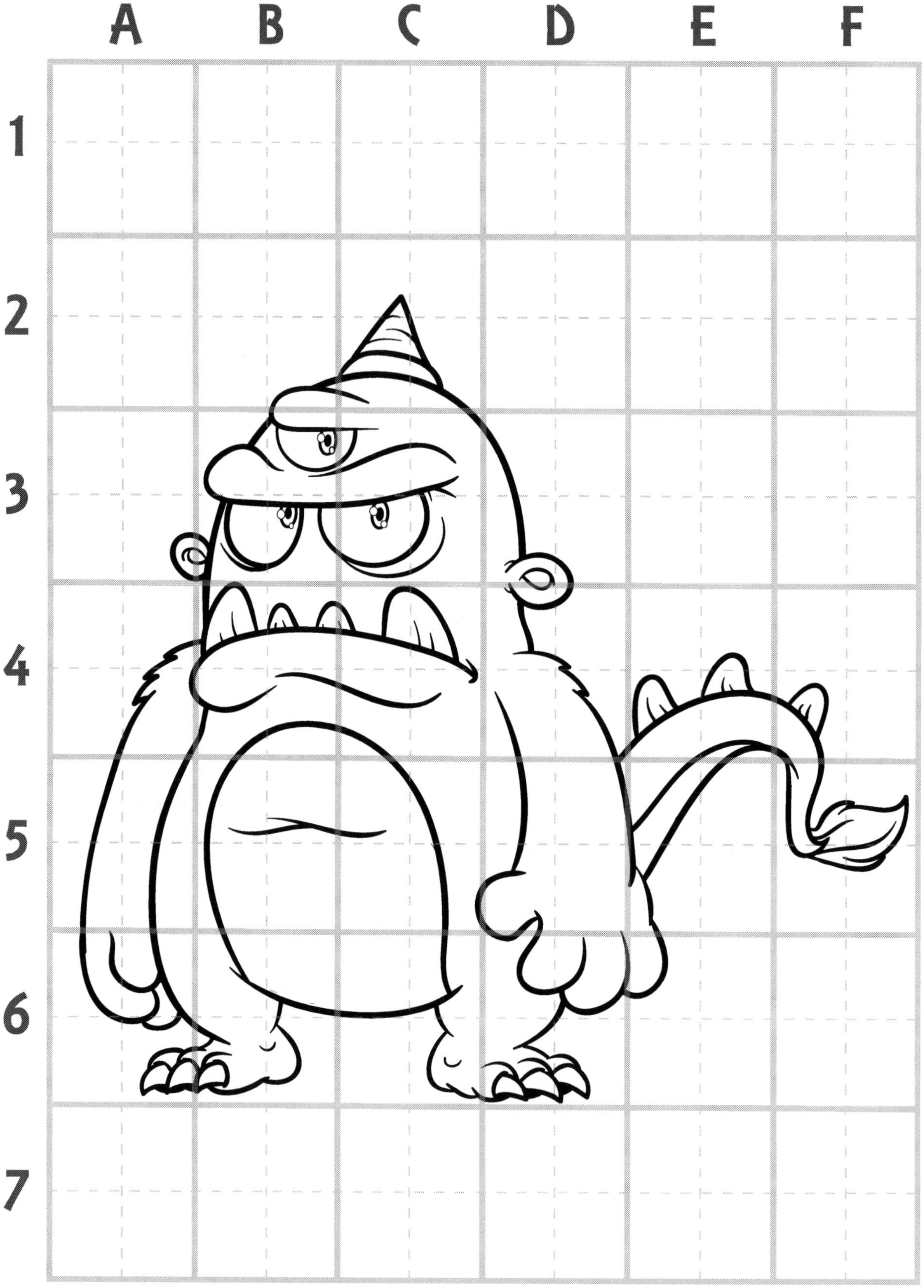
A B C D E F
1
2
3
4
5
6
7

YOUR TURN

	A	B	C	D	E	F
1						
2						
3						
4						
5						
6						
7						

TRACE IT

FREEHAND PRACTICE

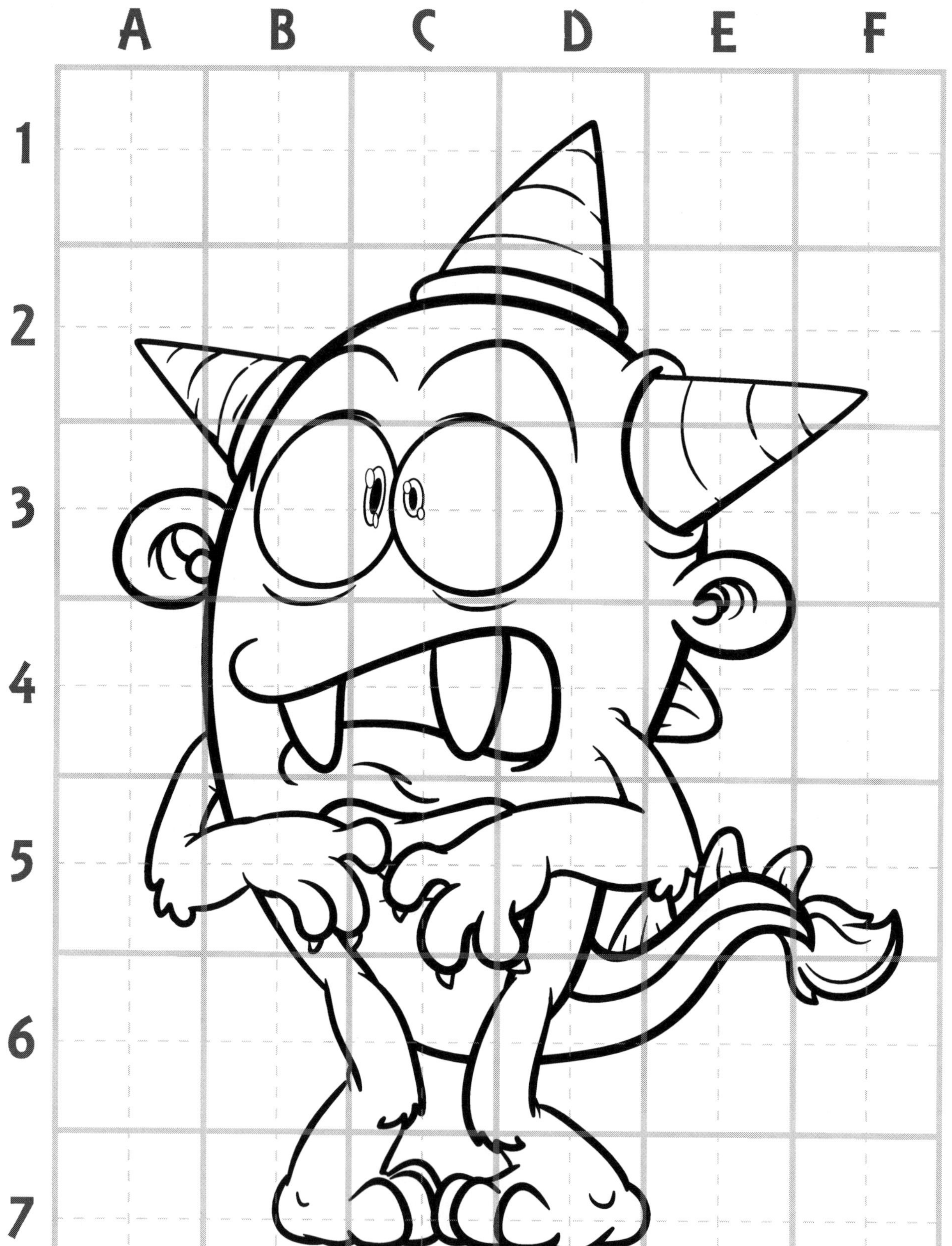
A
B
C
D
E
F
1
2
3
4
5
6
7

YOUR TURN

	A	B	C	D	E	F
1						
2						
3						
4						
5						
6						
7						

TRACE IT

FREEHAND PRACTICE

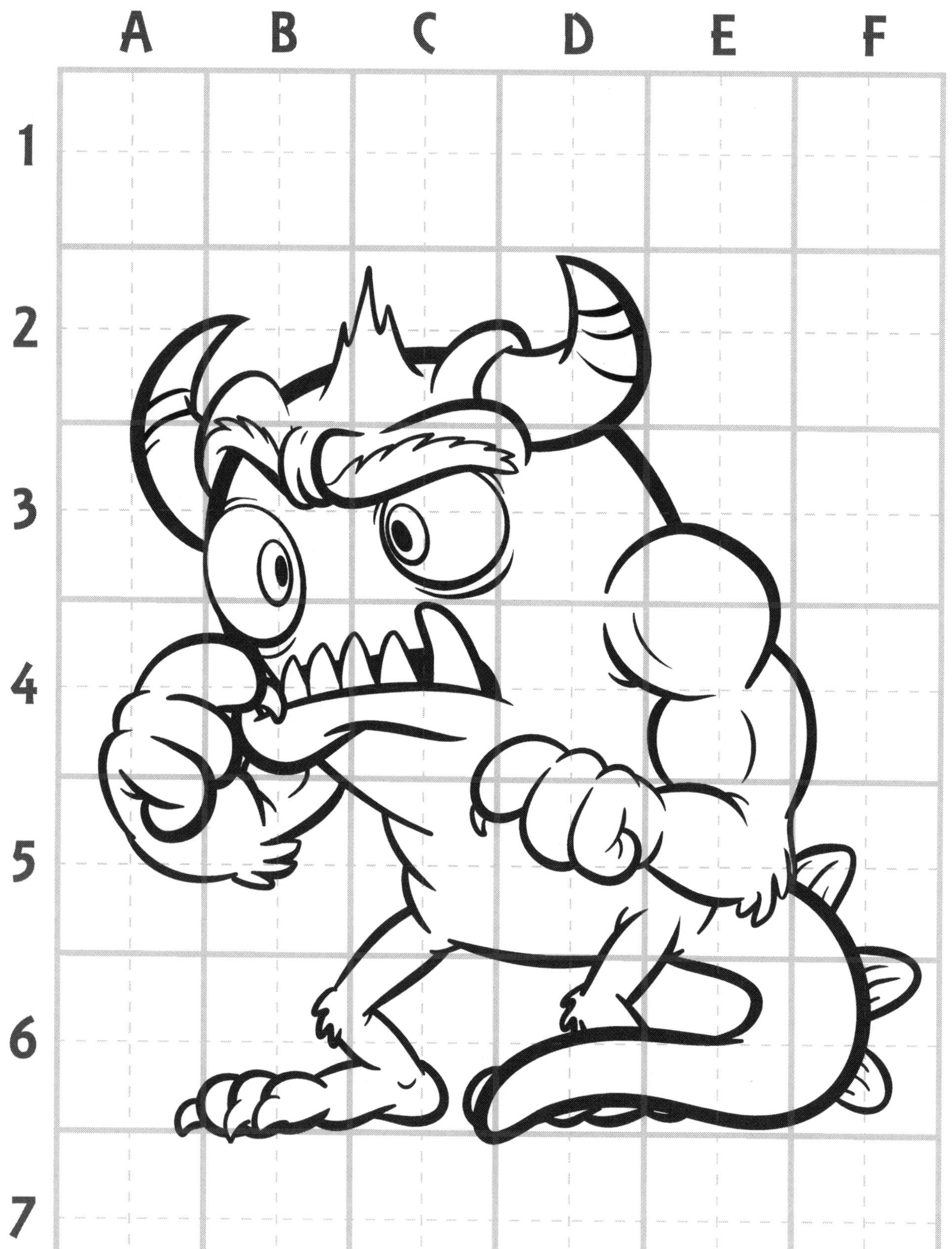
A B C D E F
1
2
3
4
5
6
7

YOUR TURN

	A	B	C	D	E	F
1						
2						
3						
4						
5						
6						
7						

TRACE IT

FREEHAND PRACTICE

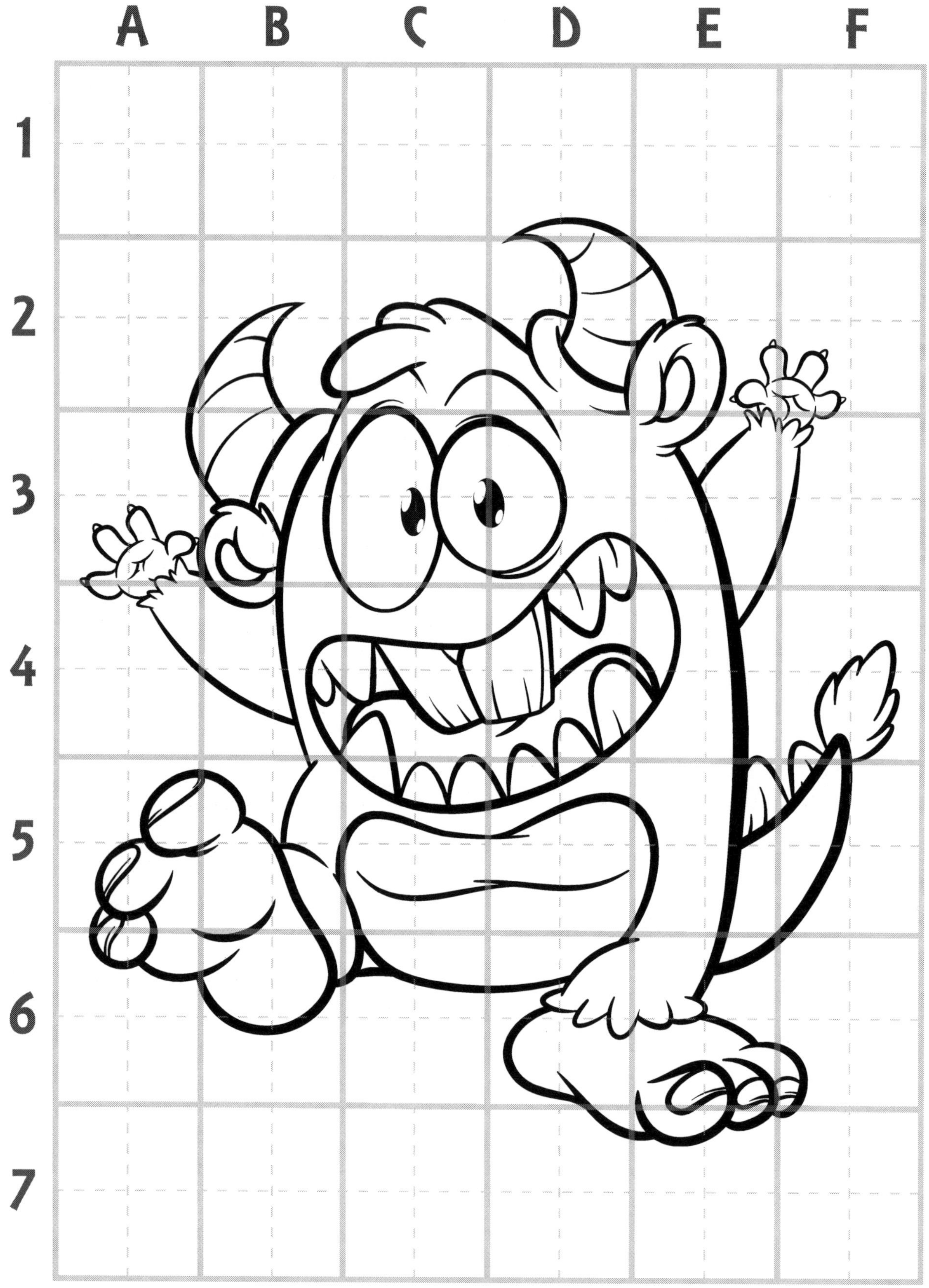
A
B
C
D
E
F
1
2
3
4
5
6
7

YOUR TURN

	A	B	C	D	E	F
1						
2						
3						
4						
5						
6						
7						

TRACE IT

FREEHAND PRACTICE

A B C D E F
1
2
3
4
5
6
7

YOUR TURN

	A	B	C	D	E	F
1						
2						
3						
4						
5						
6						
7						

TRACE IT

FREEHAND PRACTICE

PRACTICE

	A	B	C	D	E	F
1						
2						
3						
4						
5						
6						
7						

PRACTICE

	A	B	C	D	E	F
1						
2						
3						
4						
5						
6						
7						

PRACTICE

	A	B	C	D	E	F
1						
2						
3						
4						
5						
6						
7						

PRACTICE

	A	B	C	D	E	F
1						
2						
3						
4						
5						
6						
7						

PRACTICE

	A	B	C	D	E	F
1						
2						
3						
4						
5						
6						
7						

PRACTICE

	A	B	C	D	E	F
1						
2						
3						
4						
5						
6						
7						

PRACTICE

	A	B	C	D	E	F
1						
2						
3						
4						
5						
6						
7						

PRACTICE

	A	B	C	D	E	F
1						
2						
3						
4						
5						
6						
7						

PRACTICE

	A	B	C	D	E	F
1						
2						
3						
4						
5						
6						
7						

PRACTICE

	A	B	C	D	E	F
1						
2						
3						
4						
5						
6						
7						

FREEHAND PRACTICE

FREEHAND PRACTICE

FREEHAND PRACTICE

FREEHAND PRACTICE

FREEHAND PRACTICE

FREEHAND PRACTICE

FREEHAND PRACTICE

FREEHAND PRACTICE

FREEHAND PRACTICE

FREEHAND PRACTICE

Made in the USA
Monee, IL
15 November 2021

82162735R00090